Ghosts

Ghosts

by
Fred Cogswell

Ottawa, Canada
2002

Canada

*The Publishers acknowledge the financial assistance
of the Government of Canada through the Book Publishing
Industry Development Program (BPIDP)
for our publishing activities*

National Library of Canada Cataloguing in Publication Data

Cogswell, Fred, 1917-
    Ghosts / Fred Cogswell

Poems.
ISBN 0-88887-216-X

    I. Title.

PS8555.O3G5 2002   C811'.54   C2002-903528-7
PR9199.3.C64G5 2002

Cover design by Bull's Eye Design, Ottawa
Typesetting by Chisholm Communications, Ottawa
Cover photo by Dr. Malcolm Miller

Printed and bound in Canada on acid-free paper

Contents

T.V. WATCHER

Soft in her chair she sees the visions bloom
And needs no prince to wake her drowsy flesh.
Soft on the screen she sees the patterns mesh
Of rugged males whose scowling passions loom
With two-gunned violence in her living room.
Oh, how she loves them, aches to share their throes,
Her feelings sharp and variable as those
Who move in monochrome a switch can doom,

She will not flick it off for flesh and blood.
Where can she give so little, gain so much,
Be heroic without risk, diet without food,
Adventure safely in the bleak outdoors,
Have lovely children without household chores,
And thrill to love untarnished by a touch?

I Have No Need

I have no need to grieve your body gone.
This much I know now. Death is not distress
And you are here for me to rely on
In myriad ways I could not even guess –
Yet miraculous for me to bless –
The times I live are too full for sorrows
And in your death I find no emptiness
So memory becomes new life and grows.

I have no need to grieve your body gone.
Body bulk has not diminished excess
Of spirit engaging my attention
With fewer distractions to express,
Much smaller prohibitions to suppress
And more silence for poetic sorrows.
In your death I do not find emptiness
As memory becomes new life and grows.

I have no need to grieve your body gone
Because I feel the overwhelming press
Of the truest spirit that I have known
Who watches now to save me from the stress
That often causes writers' hopelessness,
Saying, "You've lost the thorn but kept the rose.
With you, pain can be no more than body's dress
And memory becomes new life and grows."

I have no need to grieve your body gone;
Adele, one needs no thorn who has a rose.
Happiness with you need not be alone
As memory becomes new life and grows.

THE CRYSTAL MOMENT

for the passing of desire, do not mourn;
it, like a rainbow, is perpetually reborn

but oh, the crystal moment which you took,
that shaped and held the flame before it broke

its shards lie shattered on a dusty shelf
deep in the cluttered store-room of your self

EVERY WRINKLE ...

Every wrinkle on my face – I've a few –
Is not paid for by time. Intensity
Puts its scars on everything I do
And I more than suspect worry will be
A serious threat to longevity.
Most people look at me as if they knew
What I did once or what was done to me:
"I wouldn't want to live what he's been through."

Every wrinkle in my mind – I've a few –
is not caused by the thought's inconsistency
But by the absent-minded things I do
And I know my lack of worry will be
A case of idle care for such as me,
So I keep my laziness now in close view:
"He thought well once till, no longer fat-free,
He found active life to sleep through."

Every wrinkle in my soul – I have a few –
Is caused when spirituality
Is threatened by solid things that I view
As limits to what should or should not be,

For they defy my rationality
With what my own subconscious always knew:
Their painful scantiness is really me
Too thin a sap to form a well-spiced brew.

Great Prince, whether indeed, thought or spirit
The life that takes you is under shadow.
Give thanks for whatever that will bear it
And in your own style learn how you should grow.

OLD-FASHIONED JOYS

After the French of Lorraine Diotte

The animals have drunk
The wood is split
The oil lamp is full
The bread is made
The children have left for school
The sky has stars.

AIR

Apart from what it does for me the air
Is blessed for being air. I see it white
On far off peaks. My eyes find solace there
From dancing rays when speed or form unite.
Unlike the earth, I cannot see my plight
In it, for, dazzled by its soft array,
Uncrushed, over the slow blot of night
My eyes achieve the clarity of day.

The things it falls on are dirty, but air
Itself is clean and fit to carry light,
Putting shining energy everywhere.
On distant peaks we look on it as white.
Its life is nearly massless in its flight
And squanders in its own and unwilled way
Colours which worldly artists draw delight
From as they fashion weeds along the way.

But the thing I love most about the air
Is that it is just like me. It is light
and whatever shape it has it must bear
The mindless blast of alien might
That makes history. When it shines most bright
Unless alone and as with it I play
Its exercise makes me a true acolyte
Of moving worshipers on a hallowed way.

Prince, the mortal tie between life and air
Is immortal. It is the world's array.
Most flexible out in the open where
All energy blesses night and day.

HAIKU

wind-blown daffodils
wink in a water-blue bowl
goldfish light the pool

I Tottered Down The Road

I tottered down the road where once I walked
But life beside it did not look the same.
I saw little of it and still less talked.
In new venue, age had staked its claim
And outside me even has altered the game
To the inner world I had ignored too long.
In that state I have ignorance to blame.
Without a tune how can one sing a song?

I whispered in the air where once I talked
But those who had heard me put in their claim:
"Your whisper can too easily be mocked
Its diction is too powerless and tame."
I take a breath: "Can air be a thing to blame?"
Inside my weary lungs the rales were long
And a fit of wheezing filled my breast with shame.
Without a tune how can one sing a song?

It's hard to be when your jaws are half-locked.
At times I ask myself, "What is your name?"
So far that question's easily unlocked
Though somehow its meaning is vague and lame.
But what then am I and whom can I blame
Without any answer given right or wrong?
O must I make a matter out of shame?
Without a tune how can one sing a song?

Since that first day when together we walked,
Prince of flat places that own right or wrong,
I've longed for a key to have this unlocked,
How can one tune a world that has no song?

His Words

Although he broke no laws
And his actions were refined,
His words combined to cause
Satyriasis of the mind.

THE DOUBLE-HEADED CHILD

A child who did not know what thunder meant
But was thrilled to breathe electric air,
I ate up books in bites of wonderment,
A feat too fast for flesh and mind to bear.
I did this alone with no one to share
The emotions that unlooked for actions fed
And in concoctions that I felt bizarre
Downed two worlds and loved the one I thought dead.

A child naive in his astonishment
And quite ignorant of any elsewhere,
I saw my neighbours and what they did went
By too habitual for me to care.
Some were like me but most would never dare
To let new things contaminate the head.
When they did they would cry "Beware, beware!"
And close their vacant eyes in holy dread.

A child who saw two worlds at once was sent
Between old routine and new nightmare,
Making dual thought a heavy torment
And psychic clumsiness a cross to bear.

When no one knew what should be kept or shed
Nor whether the key word should be"weed" or "tare"
In that melange of what's alive or dead
The anarchy I drew was my despair.

Prince, my confusion set no precedent
And too many things it did brought dismay.
Now I am old and far from the event
I'm glad I earned it in such a hard way.

BIRTH
After the French of Cécile Cloutier

Perfect from the start
That small cell
Contains
Already
The wrinkles and death
Of an old man

PAIN

I never tried to put out pain
That twisted muscles in your face
And filled your sunshine-eyes with rain,
Twisting your lips to a grimace.
I was not cruel but I could not face –
When it could be seen – the glad glow
That first arrived to fill the space
Without which it could never grow.

I did not try to ease the pain.
Shame's grief was too strong to erase
All my ardours over again.
For the first time and the first place
Light laughter caught me in the face.
It hit my pride and hurt it so
That I was frozen in disgrace
Too much even to let her know.

To build a pain can kill a pain.
I know this now but as I trace
My life I find a softer strain.
Rejection offers me a newer race

When at a sedate slower pace
Some peace through time at last can flow
Unclogging in more even grace
When love at last subdues ego.

Prince, peace is life as much as pain.
Whatever moves may move so slow
That first and last will rise again
As round and round our efforts go.

APOCALYPSE

After the French of Pierre Chatillon

An angel
like winged sunset
drowned itself
in the sea.
In this way
night descended
upon existence.

POSSIBILITIES

Possibilities were strong when
The winds of imagination blew;
Almost I thought them real. Only then
After I tried to touch somewhere I knew
All was an illusion nothing could get through.
With a numbness transcending hot and cold.
For the first consciousness since breath I drew
I did not need a mirror to be old.

Possibilities were strong when
Parts of me did the things they used to do;
Raising hope for motive and meaning then
Before collapsing to mere déja vu.
I shall not count the times when hope withdrew.
To take away the end destroys the gold
In any game where interest drew
The meaningless of money to the old.

Possibilities were strong when
Life was liquor that time could never brew
Nor a space contain. In this case a pen
Is impossible and if that be true
Anarchy closes ways to think and do
For which our energies are bought and sold,
Ending all worry dependent on view
And removing its stigma from the old.

Great Prince, in this verse I mean me and you.
Take away words. Life's easier controlled
And size can depend only on the view.
What matters if we are now young and old?

LENS

I own a lens of mystery
Unbound by light or size
Where cells inside my brain
Take life by surprise.
Of it I won't complain
For there my interest lies.
It is clear to me
When I see what I want to see
After I close my eyes.

If miracles can be
Wonder will make me wise.

Do Not Worry About A Circumstance

Do not worry about a circumstance
That alters ways to fit the grooves you've found
It matters more to feel with any dance
All the rhythms as they glide round and round.
Place is place, but energy is profound
Wherever light is. Its motion's unfurled.
Make individual steps cover ground
As a melange of atoms tunes the world.

Don't ever try to change a circumstance.
Any altered speed at all can be found
Relative to both the size and the prance
Of what it is; how far away's the ground
These things determine what rhythms rebound
As what's in and around us sounds are swirled.
You can't tell a real noise from a rebound
But an echo can represent the world.

Don't ever try to avoid circumstance
For on this earth deafness does not abound,
But see with more than eyes the lights that glance
And hear the undertone where echoes' ground

Makes gravel out of a much lighted mound,
And then enjoy. Enjoy sheer being curled
And take whatever residue is found
When smaller things than atoms tune the world.

What we call wisdom is much more than chance
And quality is not a jewel impearled.
There is, good Prince, no rank in circumstance;
The best name for anarchy is the world.

TWENTIETH-CENTURY QUESTION

After a hundred years you have a place
Whether in a small tribe or vast nation.
What was it enabled you in your case
To survive a planet's devastation?

DICHOTOMIES

Sometimes what's gone will not return again
Even if the world wants it to be as
Active as the accompanying brain.
Rachel's love must die in part like Leah's;
Both of them depend on panaceas.
Although our feeling ducts stay young and kind,
And cry real tears for abstract ideas
An old body can't keep up with its mind.

Sometimes what is over may be a strain
When for a short time bodies seem to be as
Keen to feel their life-thaw return again.
Then remember that no panaceas
Can equal unity, no ideas
Can break it down. Great love's completely blind;
Thought can't create a living there just as
Old bodies can't control an unshaped mind.

Before consciousness, unity was plain,
Inside the womb. There were no ideas.
Other worlds had to explore and gain.
Fancy was everywhere. Panaceas

Then afflicted our units forced to live as
A hodge podge of the free and the confined;
In such a case there is no unity.
No old body can fit a timeless mind.

I wrote this poem, Prince, so you can see
What now I know but had not known before,
An old body and a mind cannot be
Summed up by simple words like "either", "or".

LIVING

After the French of Maurice Champagne

"Life, my lad,"
Said the moon to me,
"Is as clear as death."

From Too-Close Colleagues ...

From too-close colleagues and a detached Chair
The staff ignores everything I say.
Non-being in a stale and stagnant air
Is an academic gift of back pay
For one who on any less formal day
Gets his own back by just being human.
For me it is an easy thing to bear
And ends up in making me a new man.

With too-close colleagues and a detached Chair
The staff can drone and hum its normal way.
I can shut my eye-lids, forget they're there
And relax with darkness. Let fancies play
In a warmer world that allows free sway.
Electric lights can't define the human,
But democratic darkness cannot bear
Light that limits whom we need to view man.

With too-close colleagues and a detached Chair
The irony of joy can hold full sway
As we learn darkness is a haven where
The free mind can expand itself in play

And seize on bliss that more than eyes convey.
Warm-feeling in the dark's more than human
And brings intensity no light can bear
From the primal world, eons ere the new man.

With too- close colleagues and a detached Chair,
Prince, we find an old lost world again. There
In darkness we are compelled to view man
In the variety of what's human.

IMMORTAL PLOWMAN

His footsteps wavered
in the clay, but each furrow
that he turned was straight

HEAD OF A FAUN

After the French of Arthur Rimbaud

Spotted with gold in the arbour's green cage
Is leafage that blossoms uncertainly
As a fine flower waits a kiss to engage,
Alive and deadly to embroidery.

A frightened Faun opens eyes to behold
And bites the red blossoms with his white teeth;
Bloody and tanned, like wine that is old,
His lips laugh out through the birches beneath.

And after he fled – like a scared chipmunk –
His laughter in the leaves still tumbles on.
See, scared by a bullfinch that caused his fun,
The wood's "gold kiss," in confusion has withdrawn.

WORLDLY WISDOM

The wise men never count
The gifts they give away
In which case their amount
Can vary day by day

But wiser men of thrift
Will never let us see
The value of their gift,
Intangibility.

THERE ARE STRANGE CONCURRENCES TO SCAN

There are strange concurrences to scan
By all those who in appearances trust
Where both the artist and the policeman
Can find themselves delighted by a bust.

VALE

There isn't much left that we could say to
Each other after all the things we've done.
It's hard to see how we found the way to
Remember the paths long ago begun
Which, however we tried, did not make us one
But forged feelings that both respected
For their narrow depth. Love wasn't really fun
But a nobler thing than we expected.

Habit is not a hard force to give way to;
Lighter when it starts a downhill run.
As time passes it's easier to pray to
Priapus and expect more from what is won
Unless the god alone controls the gun,
In which case, what each of us suspected
Becomes – like a marriage to a nun –
Divinity in mind – love aspected.

What I have written down here are words I say to
Prove I am not so wise as Solomon
Although my hair is biblical, grey to
Suggest a weakness that betrayed Sampson

(Were he bald what could Delilah have done?)
Love can be a purity long respected,
But when it's gone words must supply the fun,
Harder to put down, easily rejected.

Prince, I write when I can no longer run,
But don't think these words are utterly vain.
They can produce a modicum of fun
That may drown out a long silence of pain.

WHAT WILL BE?

After the French of Michel Beaulieu

What will this tender month be?
What buds bleed in sunlight?
What will this week be
When birds fly back from the south
In a sharp pointed triangle?
What will this day be
When the last snow turns black
In blocks, day faded green shapes?
What will this night be
When I recognize in its very sediment
Your face?

IN WAR

After the French of Alphonse Piché

Left, right, left right, from home we've fled,
Little soldiers in big commands.
Left, right, left right, as our boots tread
All through strange and far-away lands.
Bones are left now as time commands.
For stews whose smells are strong to fall
On grand-sires and sires who plant dead hands
With people worth nothing at all.

The battalion's light right now is dead,
Killed by marsh and rot. In those sands
Where grapeshot normally was sped
Among bombs unaccompanied;
One will see men's guts move through their hands
Like robots unceremonial;
Another will rummage earth's lands
With people worth nothing at all.

Left, right, left right, when we have fled
From our military commands;
Left, right, left, right, and in our stead

Put old shoes of our reprimands
For mishaps on our asphalt strands.
Whatever is left to befall
We shall see that our lot now stands
With people worth nothing at all,

Wounded, broken, poor devil, vet,
What you forgot you now recall
And take up your position yet
With people worth nothing at all.

LOVE

... as he rushed toward
her outstretched arms, his toe crushed
a ground-sparrow's nest.

THE RISING OF THE SUN

After the French of Sully Prudhomme

Plunged in royal ennui, the burning sun
In a desert of skies silently nears,
Scatters and restores to chaff anyone
From the grave, far-off choir of spheres.

Hung in the abyss it's not high or low.
It takes from me flame, the fire of its rays.
It looks neither up nor moves down below
But the world is gilded by its new-old gaze.

Flamboyant, invisible to blandishment
It fathers wheat as wheat enlarges portals
But offers no weight to the corpulent
In troops of too heavy haughty mortals.

Among the black globes, it purples and leads
Livid depths as cold as the airy blues.
The earth submits to it the curve it needs
And seeks its course in a maze of its views.

Its flexible axe now offers the day
Enormous thickness and a living force
And the fields and trees come to share the way,
Held in by an eternal moving course.

But scattered men never do have long strides.
Inside their own soil they plunge or come back.
When sleepers go out to find that light glides
The others in the dark stretch and contract.

Ah! the sun's sons where each East-eye leads,
Admiring the place where their old glories die,
Crying: "Hail to the gods where four great steeds
Strike with a silver foot the thick red sky."

Now we cry out to Infinity: "Hail,
The Great All," tools' idol, Temple, priest.
We offer a place in a cosmic jail
Like the earth to the moon falsely at least.

It has fallen, that marvelous curtain,
Where the real world for its illusion gropes.
Science has conquered our eyes, uncertain
Man has repudiated his vain hopes.

Reason has owned up to its lying of old.
We've tasted its pillars exceedingly.
It seemed more staple, sustaining its hold
As the whole universe clothes fresh beauty.

HALF-WAY HOUSE

There is a half-way house in memory
As unwanted death accommodates grief
By attention and forgetfulness
That allows routine as a compromise
To keep up hope for another future
And bring its rotting seeds a better life.

But when can I look for such things in life?
Not in the winds of ruined memory
That feel fresh chaos within its future
And worship the intensity of grief.
I find but little joy in compromise
And a coward in forgetfulness.

But when I think of it, that forgetfulness
Is an inner thing, and its cancelled life –
Although a more honest tie than compromise –
Is a false worship of self-memory
In which deception is the soul of grief
While a dried ritual proclaims the future.

Remembered or forgotten, the future
Is only an anthropological mess
Not strong enough to merge with any grief,
More of a statistic than a life
Like a wavering wind of memory
Or the slow stagnant pool of compromise.

In the world I knew there's less compromise
In working with no thought for the future
Or to depend upon the memory
As what we do, replete in its fulness,
Fuses with our whole being. That is life.
Its demands swallow us beyond belief.

Who was it said: "Art is long. Life is brief"?
Such a one gave himself no compromise.
A task outside himself drained him of life
As he found that patterned creativeness
In a form without killing its true life
Was the one straight path to eternity.

In this verse six words direct patterns: *life,*
Compromise, forgetfulness, memory
Leaving no room for *future* or for *grief.*

COULD I ...

Could I make my love art
To last till time is stayed
I would carve a red heart
And two clear eyes of jade.

Could I make my love last
In time and space with me
Not a fig for art I'd give.
I would not carve but be.

ACT OF LOVE

After William Shakespeare

Although the speech between us lies immense
There floats across the void from him to me
The fine-spun gossamer of poetry
Drawn from the entrails of experience.

Not like a web that catches flies by chance
And lets them wither to oblivion;
This is an act of love whose touch is one
With all of mind and muscles nervous dance.

A Trojan plain, the sound of martial drums.
A withered crone, face torn by grief or fear
Amid the press of Grecian victory.
No need to ask the question now: "What's he
To Hecuba that he should weep for her?"
I read, and in my tears the answer comes.

WE WILL NOT SLOW DOWN

We will not slow down; then, the guilt
Would be much greater since a full
Acquaintance with the beautiful
Would remind us of walls we built.

Bleed self-wounds to their very hilt
And cut through red-nerves to the rind
Till in our view romance is blind
And wonder-gold has died to silt.

We each in flesh and spirit bear
One such individual life
Whose outside surface is a knife
Designed to guard us everywhere.

But close inside a world of care
As we sort through confusion's maze
We feel a knife can cut two ways
But do not find a solace there.

SEASONS

After the French of Nicole Brossard

I shall homeward steer
like vines when they go
in the Spring of the year
one with the night's glow.

I shall do the flame's dance
in patterns fine
as Summer's light glance
makes all movement shine.

I shall leave now
against the burnt land
to complete my vow
on the dizzy sand.

I shall land alone,
a desert island own
in the sudden epoch
of a new shock.

IT BEGAN IN 1935

It began in 1935 when
Dr. Wellington Koo addressed the Normal School
Students of Fredericton. I listened
To China's representative at the League
Of Nations. What I heard him say expelled
From me what I thought was education.

At that time Saxe Rohmer was education
About the Chinese but Koo killed it when
His eloquence that childlike myth dispelled
Before his speech had begun. In the school
Library I then found and read a big
Book, *The Importance of Living*, and listened.

But not long after that time I listened
To another facet of education
That touched on ideas of a greater league
And provided me a real break-through when
I read *Sayings of the Old Boy*, a school
of tenets which my mind has since then held;

In other words, Lao Tsu, however spelled.
Two forces were its key. To both I listened
And the two together provided school
To a more rational education.
Out of opposites came complements when
Yin and Yang together created league.

And what ideas were, so life was. League
Became the deepest principle I held
And which held me. Things grew easier when
I learned the old life of new things, listened
to the recurrent course of education
Though this was not inherent in school.

In *either-or* most of us found a school,
Though opposites can dissolve any league
And destroy the basis of education.
For years now to these I have not listened.
Words like "Yes" and "no" my mind has dispelled
In favour of spurs like "what", "why", and "when".

Inside any league, inside any school –
A good recipe for education
Is to follow what's easier to spell
Or listen to, words like *whose, what, where, and when.*

The Clear Morning Of Spring

It is the clear morning of Spring
And the sap is oozing out of its pores
In the tree-trunks cast down and left behind
By loggers in good days the year before,
And there a badly mangled butterfly
Recalling honey is moved to sip it down.

A ruined place whose branches have broken down
And still unmelted snow holds back the Spring
And would hold life to try a butterfly
Pouring its blood down the thickened pores
In almost a last gasp effort before
A snapped bent bough left inertia behind

And, as if released by a puff of wind,
There on a tree's mossed bust it settled down
And let me see its clarity before
Any of its movements obscured the Spring.
So clear it was that through all the pores
Of its fine lines I saw the butterfly.

It was for me the year's first butterfly.
I was not one to keep dates on my mind
But when I saw light rays through living pores
It was the true beginning of my year
And the moment when I was touched by Spring
Was the climax I'd wanted long before.

You must discover ways of light before
Despite the adage "When it rains it pours"
You realize that true light has filtered down;
The glory that's inside you won't be behind
And if its life can rouse a butterfly,
Once it's begun, no one takes back the Spring.

Now the build-up starts. Both the hart and hind
Try to abate their frenzy and bring down
The fire of all their heated blood before
Strength that kept their going throughout the Spring
Loses energy which inflames their pores
Whether they walk, or crawl, or swim or fly.

Before, behind, up, down, in light that pours,
The harbingers of Spring are never blind.
Make way now, for a living butterfly.

BEFORE THROWING THE ANCHOR
After the French of Clarence Comeau

O my love, whenever I draw your face
The ink is flowing over deep silences.
My anguish stretches long as your body.
Your mouth repents its thoughts in October.

You reappear everywhere I am we.
My gaze traverses the dreary landscape.
We resemble an Autumn that freezes
The last long days of a gathering in.

All comes back in this difficult poem.
Nothing lets me forget its small memory.
If you wished I would become every word
That we would have used in our time of love.

These winds in tresses of a blond country –
O my love, whenever I draw your face
Borne away on the sea of overthrow
You reappear everywhere I am we.

A COSMIC QUESTION

Slowly in its stillness the shadows made
A deeper image in their muffled shapes
From the vague monochromes of denser dawn
As the world I was used to see became
Light-filled and alive in intensity
Where cracked rays create lines to form patterns.

Cracked rays created lines to form their patterns
Until clouds destroyed what their lustres made
And drowned them in wet intensity
Deadly to the anatomy of shapes.
In this way the world a lead lump became
And lingered close to blackness until dawn.

Since the earth's first backwater was the dawn
And in its confused movements all the patterns
Were two-way invaders, as they became
Part of a war or a love-affair made
Between beings opposite inside their shapes
All were attracted by intensity.

To end stability, intensity
Is necessary. What occurs at dawn
Becomes an exotic touching which shapes
Two mysterious ironic patterns
That their new and first acquaintance made,
A double lure that both of them became.

It is ironic that what both became
Must much redouble their intensity
And bring real meaning to their efforts made.
As things develop, war or peace at dawn
Can never end the struggle. These patterns
Are permanent and must not double shapes.

It takes small things like these to create shapes
And grow and feed the monsters that became
Who found that difference can make patterns
Endowed with much too much intensity.
There cannot be an armistice at dawn
In the green world animals have made.

What use to keep alive the shapes we had
Whose intensity destroys the dawn
In the queer world our restless brains have made?

MY HEART

After the French of Alfred Desrochers

My heart is a forty-eight year old ancestor
Where sons have become defunct and whose wife
    has died.
"How weak is spirit, how often have the sense lied?"
He muses, hunched over the threshold of his sagging
    door.

He prates empty hope to the visitor
What the present offers the future gives;
His sleazy hovel where the sow-bug lives
Is the sum of his powerful labour

But he goes each day to wander the shore
And, peering afar, haunted by dreams of old,
Often before his eyes he his hand propels

To watch if, coming back from adventure,
He did not see before glorious vessels
His captain sons, upright, harnessed in gold.

A Liaison

For a few hours in the evenings
he often goes to see her

and she sits with her sewing
while he sits smoking his pipe

sometimes when their eyes meet
they smile in the happy silence

so much at one they are
it does not really matter
that their bodies must not touch.

On a Broken Marble

After the French of José Maria Heredia

The moss is pious. It lets sad eyes close.
In feral woods it now hunts in vain for
The Virgin who Her pure milk and wine will pour
On earth where good names their limits impose.

Today hops, ivy, viburnum, a rose
To roll themselves around divine debris,
Not knowing if Pan, Faun, or Mystery
On their scared brow twisted a green nose.

See how an oblique ray, caressing it,
On its snub-nosed face makes two gold eyes run
And the silly vine laughs, each orb a slit.

And – floating glamour – on winds rough and odd,
Leaves, shifting shadows, the wandering sun
From ruined marble build a living God.

INNOCENT DREAMS

After the French of Corrine Mallais

My childhood memories are kept in my storehouse
    of remembrance.
Sometimes I open the door and secretly go inside it
To find again the garments which were accessories
To games we made up during the rainy days.

A thousand and one things transformed themselves
    at our command.
Old rags were used as medical uniforms
And pink candles as medicine.
Sometimes we played school and sometimes we even
    played house.

When good weather came back again we went outside.
We chased about the meadows breathlessly hot on
    one another's heels
And when we were too tired we took a break.
Stretched out on the grass we watched the clouds
And looked for beguiling shapes among them.
When we shook with laughter, all smiles
And far off, the adults looked at us with envy
As if dreams were only permitted to children.

We made swords out of old branches.
Most of our wars took place at that time
And they always ended by tiring us out.

Seated in my old armchair I realize sadly
That all those games were only dreams and all those
    dreams were only games,
That war exists in reality,
And that our medicines that ought to heal an ox
No longer have a place, faced with serious illness,
Like the cancer that will come one day to destroy
A friend's youth and finally his life.

Our breathing is no longer what it was then
When we ran after one another in the meadows
For whole days without ever getting winded,
And since that time I have come to understand the
    looks of adults
Who already know the world of dreams
Belongs to children.

SO LONG ...

After the French of Raymond Breau

Flowing streams and cunning
And an all-seeing lad
Who condemns the sinning
Of an age gone to bad.

A youth who is going to replace
The errors his elders allowed
With faults of a more refined grace
Better fitted for a modern crowd.

And do you know what is the view,
You who lived in another past?
Do you know why we exclude you
In order to cast you aside at last?

You don't see your child in his flesh-faring
Nor understand the revolt in his breast
With all the styles of his rebel bearing,
But ... who sowed the hate of his harvest?

GRETCHEN THE PALE

After the French of Emile Nelligan

Hers is the beauty of a Rubens contour,
The same calm majesty later belongs.
Her voice is golden as a lute when songs
On Venetian balconies their slow rhythms pour.

Her blonde hair in a cascading shower
Covers her virgin flesh like a mantle drawn;
Her step, a milk-white sigh of cool chiffon,
Could be an angel's tread at vesper hour.

She mirrors strange gold. Is she away
From Eden or from Erebus? Is she
Angel? This uncanny jewel of clay?

See her standing here, body a young tree,
A willing Venus. Beware her demon charms!
She is that Pharos who slays with marble arms.

A Co-Inspiration
After Line 1 of Gwendolyn MacEwan's "The Music"

Upon my head a thunder-storm can fall.
Never can I lose its sharp memory.
Like a sailor broken by a giant squall
I hug it close to me.

I would know nothing but flower-delight,
Yet what can make humanity more real?
And tomorrow if these wide skies grow bright
What is it they reveal?

I'll only sing, "In that place at that hour
I loved. I was loved. Beautiful was she."
I hide this in my soul but do have power
To make what God bade be."

FROM THE OTHER SIDE

After the French of Martine Jacquet

From the other side of the dark
the flowers of May blur beneath the curve
of time
and you try desperately
to climb over the wall of your childhood
and you show me how the roses
smell good in that garden
even if now you press them
between the pages of your memory-book

PERCÉ ROCK

After the French of Gonsalve Desaulniers

A cape choked by kelp and gray water's rock
North assaults have shaken it only to jail
And a dolphin passing through under the gale
Comes sometimes to rub it with tattooed back.

On its vast gap when the dark comes down
A giant shadow fills all sides' wide lines
Where all day, gilding a gulf that shines,
Along with azure, light plays with its own.

Stubborn, calm, alone, mammoth tides it flings
And its rocks, by brackish waves surrounded,
Float for centuries the most bitter breeze,

And the great gulls, stout pigeons of the seas,
Swoop and wheel, fantastic flight rounded
As they make a white song with scrawny wings.

KORE

Triptolemus, Eumulpus, and Embuleus
Walk sadly down the pasturage of dawn
By that sea-girt Eleusinian meadow
Where a half-pomegranate mocks the corn ...

To them it seemed they still might see her
As first they saw her in the April air,
A child who twinkled in a corn-green gown
With scarlet poppies bleeding in her hair.

Triptolemus, Eumulpus, and Embuleus,
Strong violent men whose passions knew no law:
A child less lovely would have been their prey,
But her eyes dissolved their lusts to awe.

Dry wizened grasses glowed beneath her feet.
Her careless touch awoke the sleeping trees.
The sunlight on her kirtle as she moved
Settled like a swarm of golden bees.

Strange light was in the clear sky of those days.
It made the air taste amber wine, and corn
Be food that fed yet left all hungers keen;
Each draught of mead was like a joy new born.

But now the sunlight cannot pierce a thin cloud.
And on the frozen meadow hard and chill
Triptolemus, Eumulpus, and Embuleus
Look on the hoofprints of the horse of hell ...

SILENCES

After the French of Jacqueline Royer

I

I   live in a silence

                night-prism

                starry cage

hammered by bursts of laughter

II

              I hear a stranger's footsteps

              familiar rumours

              taking their shoes off

              on my threshold

III

I leave silences behind
because too short, too scented
I leave them like frozen nightdresses
like a tent beating in the wind

IV
I open windows in my silence
in order to pass better the silence
of the cliffs and the lanes

V
I wear the scars
of abandoned silences

too sombre
too luminous
by means of torches on the walls

VI
I destroy
musical instruments
keeping only voice

I invent

instruments of silence.

ENOUGH

After the French of Lorraine Diotte

I've had enough of being watched
Solicited
Bled white
To satisfy your demands.
My life,
I'll give it back.
Good luck!

IXION IN HELL

"Had I pleaded love
I had not been here but I
told the truth and said:

'Pardon me, Hera –
Too much wine made me mistake
Your cloud for a bed'."

THIS PAPER ONCE BREATHED

In bud and leaf and twig
this paper once breathed

Tonight it speaks
my life in you.

ON A RAY OF LIGHT

After the French of Nicole Brossard

On a ray of light
I pad my poems
like wreathes

orbited by my horizons
I climbed over their pregnancies
sliding on an archipelago
of crazy rivers

I planted poems in my heart and guts
a good scree invented my landscape
I opened myself like an oyster under the knife
of its rainbow

pool of my stars swelling
the base of my loneliness
buoy of my reality
seabird of my desertions

I anchor myself to your creel.

THE CHAINS OF LILLIPUT

It was the chains of Lilliput
Taught Gulliver he was a giant.

OF ALL THE LINES WRITTEN ...

Of all the lines written the most crippling
Capsule upon the origin of pain
Was one used by both Chaucer and Kipling
"Dayspring mishandled comes not again."

ALWAYS I WAIT FOR THE SWEET MEMORY

After the French by André Chenier

Always I wait for the sweet memory
When, applying the flute over my mouth, he
Laughed and held me over him, near his heart,
Called me his rival, though first from the start.
He shaped my lip, unskilled almost unsure,
To a whistle harmonious and pure,
And, gripping my fingers in his hand's cover,
Lifted and lowered them, twenty times over,
Teaching them, still weak, to learn
How to close holes in the sound-box in turn.

MOTION IS MEANING

motion is meaning
a forming that slips
into and out of
a mindless dark

when from everything
each sorting being
each various *Now*
hardens to shape;

bright patterns glow
trapped on time's stone
as frail beads flash
air threaded on bone.

LIKE AN ORANGE

After the French of Jacques Godbout

When a child
Gives birth
To another child
And when the two

These two lucky children
Look at each other

The earth stops being round
In order to show them
Where to go
And it stretches out
Like an orange skin
    peeled

Overload

these modern-day prophets
speak to the young,
*Be open, expand
your mind receive send*

is it any wonder
that the young crack up?

do you know
how many trillions
of impressions
bombard each of us
on every conceivable
wavelength
during
the psychic energy
of a lifetime?

how to shut off
the screaming overload
how to handle
it in patterns
how to refrain
from adding to
the cacophony
these are essential
tricks for survival
and must be learned
early

whether or not
we like it
we are caught between
monitor and madness

AFTER YOU LEFT ME ...

after you left me I stood
silent on grey sands
and watched while a deaf
and dumb tree talked to the wind
with fluttering hands

DRAGON-FLY

After the French of Jocelyne Villeneuve

She drinks sunlight ... eggs
one hundred times forgotten
on water-lilies

CLASSROOM

a great gust of wind
bends our student heads to one
attentive level

in the yard outside
each flower steeps itself in the
silence of the sun

AFTER THE STARS

After the French of Jocelyne Villeneuve

Every night the
fireflies are reinventing
the zodiac

STILL

though quasars pierce an emptiness
six billion light years cannot hold

though light itself is trapped
in the cold of collapsed nebulae

though all of history
is dwarfed by spatial sounds

still ...

the earthworm glistens in the dew
its beauty independent of
the hunger of the bird.

SUMMER NIGHT

After the French of Emile Nelligan

A violin sings the song of grief profound,
Joined by a horn to fill the calm of night;
The Sylphids mourn the souls in tranquil flight
And the tall years' hearts emit a dying sound

As a breeze dies each leaf to life is sped
And the light twigs sway in their rhythms free.
The young birds dream; under the milky eye
Of a summer moon, no grief is harvested.

To the whispered concert by the crickets borne
These sabbath-seeking elves beneath the boughs.
In my throbbing heart echo suddenly
The distant song of all night's mystery
Whose murmurs in the lazy heaven's drowse
Pulsing until the rise of humid morn.

THERE ARE TWO WORLDS IN TIME

There are two worlds in time; one dark, one light,
In circling stasis each on other preys,
Where all between the poles of black and white
Resolve or spiral through their nights and days.

When you behold the blind and silent worm
Become a song inside a robin's throat,
Or see in Spring a fragrant orchid form
It's own sweet scent from slime that feeds its root.

Think how in turn a worm will feed as well,
One night to come, upon that robin's meat,
Or how the root that gave will cannibal
And care not if the bloom be foul or sweet.

And realize then, unlike flower, worm, bird, slime,
Your thoughts of time have put you out of time.

GYRFALCON

When that mysterious and silent bird,
the gyrfalcon, landed on the feeder
No motions could be seen. There were neither
In that fear-filled place any noises heard.

I stared at it and never said a word
As strangeness killed curiosity.
So far it was from where it ought to be
No one could ever know what had occurred.

Before the entrance door and garden wall
It did not notice anything at all
Until at last it rose and stretched its wing
Then flew for the north sky, leaving the shelf.
Too independent for a living thing
It was aware of nothing but itself.

ORAL TESTING

In my youth when it was boys' turn to speak
They had to be careful what they should say.
They had heard their teacher throughout the week
Say what they might forget on any day.

Girls were more circumspect, pretending meek.
They could reword questions to while away
Questions already asked. By this delay
Question-time to them never seemed a freak.

As a student when words said what they said
The range and volume of the books I read
Were awe-inspiring; in fact, enormous,
But words I said were too hard to get at.
They came from my mouth, maybe my palate,
And without consent made me genius.

When I Was Young And Game-Intense

When I was young and game-intense
My fancy lost its innocence.
I learned how feeble sense could be
When measured by my psyche.

I'd play a game of basketball
And hardly feel an ache at all.
Interest then would cover it
But the walk back home ... that took grit.

January Morning

... the morn-ending gold
of wind-fall dawns ... naked trees
Ermine glad in cold

SHE SAID ...

She said, "Sorrow's cup
should be measured sip by sip,"
but he drank it up

or made it bullet
as he drowned its ownership
in his own gullet.

WINTER

in another's arms
you sleep ... heavy lies the snow
on our summer bed.

POETRY IS THE LUTE OF WISDOM

After the French of Huguette Légaré

What is good for any self is to be a great master
knowing how to make words save him because he
    loves them
but does not especially favor them. That old man,
    obscure
in us, says: "Since a child leaves its mother's
womb when it is ready, how can time spent here be
    wasted?"

Poetry is the cello, deeper than active emotions, the oboe
of lyricism, the trombone of social prophecy. Above all
else, it is the lute of wisdom.

HAIKU

coin silver on a
dark rich tablecloth, who will
pick you up, full moon?

THE SPRING
After the French of José Maria de Heredia

The soil lies beneath the thorn with grass brushed
    and dry;
And the nameless Spring which drop by drop fills a
    tomb,
With her sad song engulfs the solitary coomb
She is the Nymph, weeping an eternal goodbye.

In the slave's idle mirror that keeps its wrinkles dry
And scarce reflects the passing pigeon's wing,
Sometimes a moon that from black skies we fling
In that place alone sees the pale face of the sky.

From drop to drop an errant shepherd thirst unloads,
Drinks, and like an ancient talisman of the roads,
Lets a bit of water fall out of his hands' hollows.

Despite himself, hereditary action follows.
His eyes do not see on the tombstone there
The liberating vase of the parterre.

SINISTER RITUAL

After the French of Huguette Légaré

The forty-year-old woman who still lives with her
parents, the ones who have a big house and a heart-
shaped driveway in front of the door, is getting ready
to go out, as in every afternoon, to walk her dog
around the neighborhood on a leash.

She speaks to the servant-girl: "I think I am going
to put on my coat that does not show the dirt, my
thick-soled, hardwearing shoes, the blouse that I wore
yesterday because they are rebuilding the street and
dust is gathering."

RITE

After the French of Jocelyne Villeneuve

A second coffee ...
Down there, in a narrow lane
Sunlight sips the dew.

MIGRATION

After the French of Maurice Beaulieu (1924 –   )

I am a child here
Who has left the sun behind
Who with arms in the air
Pecks his flesh like a rind

I was wind in the sky
Night death the passers-by
The blood and water of words
And the silicon of birds

I am a child here
Who from the great sea came
Who with arms in the air
Is making earth tame

The Death Of The Poor

After the French of Charles Baudelaire

Death can console, bring life to its gates.
It can be a goal with hope its one friend:
It's an elixir which intoxicates
And leads us to roads where footsteps end.

Wherever storm or snow or frost debates
Its blackness makes the strong lightning bend
To that famous inn where the good book states:
"They will eat, sleep, and well-being attend."

An angel complete with fingers that nurse
Rebuilds the beds of the naked and poor
With sleep and the gift of dream-ecstasy.

"God-glory's here, a mystic granary;
Paternal and poor combine like a purse;
To unknown skies it makes an open door."

An Old Romantic

After the French of Emile Nelligan

Wrapped in a shawl and sheltered from the cold
In the window-sill near the pots of flowers,
Miss Adele sits at ease while her eye devours
A Dumas-novel like a twenty-year-old.

A convent of antiquities Behold
In her whose boudoir sprawls in one strange mound;
There, inlaid in her devout creed, are found
Vases, onyx, pictures, all-style books untold.

On a cushion an old Persian tomcat purrs
While the old dame squanders that heart of hers
And all its worries inside a yellowed book.

But, trapped in her fond dream, she does not see
Peer in from the street with a mocking look
A bragging orange-grinder from Barbary.

IF

After the French of Huguette Bourgois

The unbreakable skin
of your eyes
broken suddenly
allows us to see
the sea ...

WHAT LOVE SAID

What love said was true:
"I am not glue; but honey
I shall stick to you."

THE CRACKED CLOCK

After the French of Charles Baudelaire

To listen over a smoking, trembling fire
Is bitter-sweet on a winter evening,
As weak, faint memories go wafting higher
And in the fog outside far-off church bells sing.

By chance, the clock with a vigorous throat
That, despite its age, is alert, full bent
Throws faithfully forth its religious note
Like a sentinel soldier in his tent.

My soul is cracked; when with risen ennui
It wants to people air with dark distress,
It often happens that its voice, seemingly,
Draws rales from a half-forgotten wound
By a blood-lake's edge, under a great mound
Where giants strive hard and die motionless.

HOW FAR IS FAR?

How far for us is far? How past is past?
Answers to these queries are deceptive
Yet we find feelings stronger than a blast
Linked with not objects but the perspective.

No single thing can keep a value-hike
With worth too great for us to have suppressed.
Not inside itself but in what it's like
Is the deepest gold that we have expressed.

ON SAYING NOTHING
After the French of Micheline Gagnon

Let us say nothing except what first
the immortal sea-birds sang. How
their unmeasured songs will fill our voices!

SEA-BREEZE

After the French of Stephane Mallarmé

Alas, the flesh is sad and I've read all the books.
Flung down there I know the birds are drunk by
    their looks
And think themselves the unknown spume of dark skies.
None of the old gardens reflected in our eyes
Will hold both a heart so softened by the sea
That it on the paper found perfect whiteness free,
O nights! Neither the young maid who misses her child
Will ever desert a tongue whose cleanness is mild.

I shall leave, steamer; balance your masts with their foam.
Lift up the anchor so that my weird world can roam.
A boredom abandoned by cruel hopes that lie
Still believes in the handkerchief's supreme good-bye,
And, maybe, the main-masts inviting its wreckage
Are down from the heavens as wind bends its cage.
Lost, with no main-masts, nor isles to which they belong.
But, O my heart, listen to the mad sailors' song.

LAST VERSE

After the French of Alfred de Musset

Eighteen months now the hour of my decease
From all directions rings inside my ears;
Eighteen months of wide-awake ennuis
I feel them everywhere. Always this appears.

The more I quarrel with my lack of mirth,
The more I feel sickness come over me,
And when I want to set foot on the earth
My heart must stop its beating suddenly.

My great strength is never quite unbounded.
Until I rest life becomes a blast
And, like a stallion by fatigue floundered,
My weak courage reels, only to drop at last.

THE STEADY SAMENESS OF THE CHAMBER
After the French of Huguette Légaré

I am sleeping inside the outline of your hair
My haunch against the muscles of your patient thoughts
My neck upon the dreams of your sentimental and
　　turbulent groin
Adjusted by the air that comes in through the open
　　window
And I am most adaptable to your risks aesthetic and real

I have slept and I did so against the passion of your
　　hands
While waiting to go asleep between the mobility of
　　your peace
The colour of your closed eyes
The capacity for regular breathlessness from your
　　eyes' pupils
And the steady sameness of the chamber.

THE WIND AND THE TREE

That Spring the gnarled and ancient apple tree,
Feeling the May winds kiss, unfurled
Green leaves like flags to greet the sun, and all
Its crown grew white with blossom where great bees
With pollen-dusted fur flew day-long flights
To hive the harvest of the scented boughs.

Now on the Autumn ground the apples lie,
And with them soon will mingle in the mould
The leaves whose edges now are brown
With death, far deadlier than the keenest axe.
The kiss of too much living drove the tree
To greater harvest than its back could bear.

A kissing wind that did not dream its power,
A tree that could not feel the limits of
Its all too feeble strength — by chance the two
Combined. The end their union formed was fruit.
But which of us who dreams and feels can say
Whether the end of fruit be life or death?

TREASON

After the French of Nicole Brossard

I had to take hold of my heart
and shut it up in my head
under my tresses loneliness was sliding

treason

at my feet I picked it up again
ground down by passion and grief
riddled by hope and illusion

I was going to drown its stupid outcries
but I suddenly remembered
what it held

both madness and creation

ROOT

After the French of Micheline de Jordy

a shadow
sliced
by my arm's knife

a pulse of clay
the shadow spread out
on the beach –
a green lip of a rock of sound –
black sea-weed folded
on a yellow stream

the shadow
curved again
in indigo

my recreated
strength

Now's Image

One day when late Autumn harvests its crops
    I stand on a hillside where
The smell of a few burnt potato tops
    Enhances the windless air.

And in it I drink a stillness that stops,
    Like a root that needs no laws,
Whenever a crow flies over and drops
    A few unmusical caws.

Soon the soil will put an end to its sops.
    Things will stay where they are put.
Now's image is not really mud which slops
    But a hard, fresh hazelnut.

FINALE

After the French of Alfred Desrochers

My sons, I fooled myself, bringing back to you
Those skilled workers and the humble shop where
Their exploits took on an hieratic air
As shop-love transfigured them through and through.

Because inside me their image was true
I thought I held tricks to give it a glow.
Now the task dwarfs. My sonnets only show
What the footing's outlines, when blurred, can do.

I began with unwise apprenticing
I should have got you to know each fine thing
Where hands as commanders did what matters
Was like watching an elm's shadow-tatters;
Children, seeing them at work, can't escape
Their reason for life, their sense of its shapes.

PLEASURES

After the French of Jocelyn-Robert Declos

I

I am the ocean raging over
       the stripped bodies of lovers
My name is Nothing
I have wandered for millennia
       on a hummingbird sailing
       for the infinite wave of Amazons

Will you recognize me one night in the shadow
       of chestnut trees
       – after bearing pot-bellied crabs

II

I am sea-weed that stays between teeth
       after love-making

Is it surprising to be always alone
when the sea sulks without reason
The sex-less arborescence of an impure nun?

My love, these are hawthorns framed
                        by cactus
          phosphorescent and blue

III

I am the passion which reddens the naked bodies
                              of lovers
Have you recognized me, before tomorrow, mingled with
     your sweat seeking delights?

I was the unfortunate one on that planet's queue
who did not know anymore when to give
                              from the earth

I'm Surprised I Do Not Think Dreams Are Free

After the French of Alfred Desrochers

I'm surprised I do not think dreams are free
To bring the old days back to life at all
But when I do – a warning I recall –
I feel primitive saps flow easily.

If I make a faux-pas, you correct me
In the depths of myself, and thus I learn
That you have not left me and will return
After a few courses bring liberty.

Mystery of sleep and death! Not one love
Near yours is going to draw. Its chaste
Rest is when old days give us their repose.

Nothing of you that I think on can close
Except your face. Like others, it's erased
And my heart must remember it alone.

DAY TO BE RE-BEGUN

After the French of Luc Perrier

What day do you want

It awaits us on the next corner
it spies on us when darkness leaves
it has an eye on our love

was not yesterday enough
yesterday our route's hope
does yesterday no longer count

What day for today
what shall we give for it
what shall we lose for it

What is waiting for us
the day to be followed step by step
that of hunger that of thirst
that of keyless doors

It does not leave us time
to ask ourselves so many questions

It waits for us with a firm foot
it counts on us
it needs us
it will have us for sunlight
it will have us until the last laugh
it will leave us
no matter what no matter why

And it will be the one who goes away
in the background's horizon
with the light of our images
the tree that leaves us in shadow
will be the one that leaves us
with the amazement of a light
in the water on your hand or your brow

the one that will leave us
in all hope for all undivided
an eternal spark of menu

But perhaps this will be the day
that I shall recognize my hunger
my thirst for your gaze
which places itself like a star

the day when I shall have time for sunlight
in order to care without light
in order to know more truly
when your footstep
comes back to me behind me
like a perpetual refrain of bird-song

WHAT IF

What if this universe that now
So badly ordered seems
Is but the nightmare of a god
Who cannot rule his dreams?

GHOSTS

Events are ghosts that walk and make us move ...
The spider-god of history
thrives on ghosts.

Counter Blast : I

I won't respect when the race is run,
All who, after the outcome, repeat:
"Since earth has no place for losers, no one
Can ever be a hero in defeat."

Counter Blast: II

To ask "Who are terrorists?" is tacky
After Hiroshima and Nagasaki

THE OFFERING

After the French of Alfred Desrochers

O foolish virgins, who curse the Gospel today,
Sisters of my soul, wanting to dance much too soon
In a sterile amusement and leave behind their boon
Of oil to be consumed inside their lamps of clay.

They, supple, knowing all future as fragile play,
Interlace their steps to fit a rhythmic cadence;
Caring not for the moment's fleeting expense,
They postpone the vigil til the very next day.

Fraternally, these verses I offer to you
Where I am putting my past on hold, postponing
The death without joy of a youth who was too sage.

So that in our closing years we'd feel the rue
Of one who knows how to taste what the time
    would bring.
The path beyond centuries will pay your homage!

THERE WERE TWO ...

After the French of Micheline de Jordy

There were two of them
lengthened in wall-shadow
two trees dug out of hot box
dead in the blaze of a whole candle.

IT'S ENOUGH

After the French of Rina Lasnier

A pebble for grinding an insect
A hand for taming an animal
A claw for disturbing the dust
A copse for choking a brother
A closed breast for hating a child

But to destroy me, O Lord
You grind me under the rock of Christ.

AND THE COUNTRY IN RUINS

After the French of Rose Deprès

And the country in ruins?
Cost what it will
There will be devastation
Slavery will continue and storms
Will drown the seeds of survival.

Hell no longer is tomorrow,
Piled with wood; in a cat-like movement
Embers are purring
While awaiting their day.

The matches are in our hands.

MEMBER OF SCABRINI MEDIA

Quebec, Canada
2002